Manya's Dream

A Story of Marie Curie

Frieda Wishinsky

Illustrated by Jacques Lamontagne

MAPLE
TREE
PRESS

Dedication
For my friends, the scientists Selma and Arthur Zimmerman

Maple Tree Press Inc.
51 Front Street East, Suite 200, Toronto, Ontario M5E 1B3

Distributed in the United States by Firefly Books (U.S.) Inc.
230 Fifth Avenue, Suite 1607, New York, NY 10001

We acknowledge the financial support of the Canada Council for the Arts, the Ontario
Arts Council, the Government of Canada through the Book Publishing Industry
Development Program (BPIDP), and the Government of Ontario through the Ontario
Media Development Corporation's Book Initiative for our publishing activities.

Cataloguing in Publication Data
Wishinsky, Frieda
    Manya's dream : a story of Marie Curie / written by Frieda Wishinsky;
    illustrated by Jacques Lamontagne.

ISBN 1-894379-53-5 (bound).—ISBN 1-894379-54-3 (pbk.)

1. Curie, Marie, 1867–1934—Juvenile literature. 2. Chemists—Poland—Biography—
Juvenile literature. I. Title.

QD22.C8W58 2003   j540'.92   C2003-900672-7

Design & art direction: Word & Image Design Studio Inc. (www.wordandimagedesign.com)
Illustrations: Jacques Lamontagne
Photo credit: Radium Institute, courtesy AIP Emilio Segrè Visual Archives

Printed in Hong Kong

A   B   C   D   E   F

Who Was Marie Curie?

Marie Curie was the first woman to win a Nobel Prize. She won it not once but twice, and in two different areas of science: physics and chemistry. She was also the first Nobel winner who had a daughter win the prize. Irène Curie earned hers in 1935.

Marie Curie's life was all about firsts just like these. And yet, she didn't care about being first. She didn't leave her homeland, Poland, and struggle with little money in Paris just to be first. She didn't study science at the Sorbonne University just to be first. She didn't spend years looking for a new scientific element in a damp, drafty shack with her husband, Pierre, just because she wanted to be first.

Marie Curie worked and struggled because she loved science and she wanted to make a difference in the world. Sometimes she was frightened and shy, but she cared so much about her work that she took a chance and never stopped trying.

She cared so much about peace that despite ill health and a terror of addressing large audiences, she stood up and spoke out.

She cared so much about her work that despite losing her partner in science and life, she continued laboring on her projects alone.

Her work made many advances in medicine possible, especially in the treatment of cancer. It also taught scientists about the nature of the atom, enabled them to measure the age of the earth, and became an important stepping stone for new discoveries such as synthetic radium.

Her determination to pursue the work she loved, despite opposition, illness, and personal tragedy, is an inspiration.

This is her story.

"I'm not going back to that stupid school," I said, flinging myself and my books on my bed.

"Tonia," Mama said, "tell me what happened."

For a minute I looked at Mama's weary eyes and couldn't say anything. How could I complain about school when she had so much more to worry about? She worried about paying the rent, finding a better job, and qualifying as a doctor in North America.

"It's okay, Tonia," Mama said, as if reading my mind. "You can tell me. I'll listen."

"It's just that this boy Jimmy at school laughs at me. He says I'm dumb because I can't speak English well. And I have no friends. And I want to go home," I blurted out.

"But you've been at the new school for only a week. And you know we can't go back to Poland. We're starting a new life here. It will get easier soon. I promise."

"But how can you stand it?" I asked Mama. "You work so hard cleaning offices at night. You study for hours when you're home. You're always tired."

"You know what helps me?" said Mama. "A story my mama told me."

"What kind of story?" I sat up. I loved stories.

"A story about a girl who lived more than one hundred years ago in Poland. A girl who was frightened and shy, but who never gave up no matter how many hardships she faced. She had curly blonde hair that refused to stay in place, like yours. And she was stubborn and smart like you too."

"Tell me about her," I said.

"Let's go into the kitchen and have a cup of hot cocoa, and I'll tell you all about her. Her name was Manya Sklodowska."

"Manya Sklodowska," I repeated as I followed Mama to the kitchen. The name sounded familiar. Where had I heard it before?

"The world knows her as Marie Curie," explained Mama, heating hot milk in a pan. "When she grew up, she became a famous scientist who won the most important award in science, the Nobel Prize. There's a book of pictures of Poland as it looked in Manya's day in the bookcase. My mama gave it to me for my tenth birthday. Bring it here. We'll look at it together as I tell you Manya's story."

Manya Sklodowska was born at the Freta School in Warsaw on a winding street where the buildings stood side by side like soldiers. Her mother was the principal of the school. Manya was the youngest of five children.

From the time she was little, she loved three things: her family, reading and learning, and Poland. But Poland had troubles. It didn't even exist as a country any more. It had been conquered and divided into three parts like a pie, with Austria, Prussia, and Russia each grabbing a slice.

Russia ruled the city of Warsaw, where Manya and her family lived. Manya hated the Russian authorities. She especially hated their rules forbidding people to speak or read Polish or teach Polish history.

"Why can't we speak our own language?" Manya asked her parents. "Why are the Russians so mean and unfair?"

But her parents had no answers. The Russians were in charge. They could impose any rules they wanted, and the Polish people had to obey. The punishment for plotting against the Russians was jail—or even death by hanging. The simple act of teaching Polish history or reading a Polish book could get you in trouble.

It hurt Manya to see her proud father lose his job as an assistant director at the high school just because he disagreed with Mr. Ivanov, the Russian principal. That awful man even made them lose their apartment because he disliked her father and his Polish ideas. In their new apartment, they had to take in students to make enough money to live.

It wasn't fair! Why did all those noisy boys have to fill every corner of their apartment? Why did she have to get up at six to make her bed and help set the table for the students' breakfast? Why couldn't things be the way they once were, without all these strangers talking, humming, shouting, running, demanding food or help?

Day after day, Manya shut out the world and concentrated on her books. She became so good at concentrating that her family teased her about it. "You hear nothing, Manya," they said, laughing.

It was true that Manya could ignore her brother and sisters when they teased her. And she could ignore the students when they romped through the house. But she couldn't ignore the Russian authorities. She had to face the Russians day after day, especially at school.

The Russians demanded that all schools and students follow the same rules. Students could learn only about Russia and speak only in Russian.

At least at Miss Sikorska's school, Manya wasn't alone. Everyone at the school hated the Russian rules and learned to disobey them in private.

In fact, Miss Sikorska loved Poland so much that she taught her students Polish history in secret. Everyone at the school knew they were taking a big chance. If they were caught teaching or learning Polish, the school could be closed. They could be jailed or deported to Siberia, a cold and desolate region of Russia. But they loved the Polish language and history. They didn't want them to die out.

It was lucky that the janitor was helping them. Whenever Mr. Hornberg, the Russian inspector, entered the school, the janitor quickly pushed a button. Two long rings and two short rings would sound upstairs in the classrooms. Immediately, four girls would gather all the Polish history books in their aprons, race to the dormitories, and hide their books. By the time Mr. Hornberg had walked upstairs, all the girls in the class would be sewing in their seats.

One day, Mr. Hornberg insisted that one of the students answer questions about Russian history. Manya knew who that would be. Much as she hated being called on, she realized she had no choice. So she stood up in front of the Russian inspector.

"Recite the Lord's Prayer in Russian," demanded Mr. Hornberg.

Manya recited it perfectly.

"Name the last five Russian czars."

Manya named each one in order.

"List the names and titles of the people in the Russian royal family," Mr. Hornberg insisted.

Manya listed them one by one.

"Who rules over us?" he barked.

The color drained out of Manya's face. She wanted to shout, "Poland!" But she couldn't. For a minute, she couldn't speak at all.

Mr. Hornberg impatiently repeated the question.

Manya looked down at her feet. She knew what she had to say.

"His Majesty Alexander II, czar of all Russia," she said.

"Well done," Mr. Hornberg said after she had answered his final question. Then he bid the teachers good day.

As soon as he left, Manya burst into tears. All the terror and fear poured out of her, and she cried and cried.

Her teacher kissed her on the forehead. "You've done well, Manya," she said.

Manya wiped her eyes and tried to smile. Her stomach was still in knots and her knees were still wobbly, but she was glad she'd helped her friends and her school.

But Manya knew she had to leave Miss Sikorska's school the next year.

"That school is not recognized by the Russians," her father explained. "If you want to further your education, you must go to the Russian high school."

Manya knew he was right, but she hated to change schools. There had been so many changes in her life already: moving from one apartment to another; worry about money and being forced to take in students; and all the death. It had been terrible enough to lose her sister Zosia, who'd died of typhoid two years earlier. But this year her mother had died of tuberculosis, and Manya missed her so much it hurt. It was like an ache that wouldn't go away.

Why did things have to change? Why was life so cruel? Why was she forced to do things she hated?

Manya's legs felt like lead as she walked to the Russian school on her first day. There were no friendly teachers or warm hugs from her mother to make the day easier, but somehow she struggled through. It helped that she loved to read and learn. It helped that she had a good memory. But most of all, it helped to meet Kazia.

Kazia loved to laugh. Manya and Kazia giggled as they sipped lemonade and licked chocolate ices at the palace where Kazia and her family lived. Imagine: a real palace! It was like visiting a princess, although Kazia was just the daughter of the librarian to a wealthy count.

Kazia and Manya shared stories about the Russian teachers. They whispered in Polish and talked about Miss Mayer, the superintendent of students, who scolded Manya all the time. Miss Mayer especially hated her unruly blonde hair. She declared it "disordered and ridiculous," and yanked at it with a brush. But Manya's hair wouldn't be tamed. It snuck out of the tight braids Miss Mayer forced it into. She did not like Manya's disobedient hair, and she did not like her independent spirit.

How good it was to have Kazia for a friend. School wasn't half as bad now. And it was wonderful to have someone to share not only the frustrations of each day, but also dreams for the future.

"I will go to university and study science," Manya told Kazia one day.

"But, Manya," said Kazia, "girls can't go to the university in Poland. And you can't afford to go to Paris to study."

"I will go to university. You'll see. I'll study and excel. They'll have to let me go!"

And Manya *did* excel. She won the gold medal at graduation, but she still could not go to university.

Her only hope was to go abroad to Paris. But who had the money to go there? Manya's father was getting older, her mother was dead, and there were four children in the family to support. It seemed hopeless.

"Everything is a waste!" Manya felt like shouting. "All my hard work. All my dreams. All for nothing. I have no real future in Poland. How can I study science?"

Manya was in such despair that her father decided to send her to visit relatives in the country.

Manya couldn't believe it! A whole year with no studies, no responsibilities, and no Russian rules. She enjoyed every minute. For one year, she didn't think of anything except hiking, dancing, swimming, and having a good time.

But when that year was up, she had to face her future again. The choices didn't look any better than they had a year before.

"This time we can't just let things happen to us," Manya told her sister Bronya, who also wanted to study in Paris. "We have to do something to make our dreams come true."

So Manya and Bronya made a plan.

Manya, who was younger, would earn money as a governess and share it with Bronya. Bronya would use it to go to Paris and study medicine. Once Bronya was settled in Paris, she'd help Manya come. Then Manya too would have a chance to study science.

For three grueling years, Manya worked as a governess in the Polish countryside. She was lonely living with a strange family, and teaching and taking care of children was tiring and demanding work. But she had made a promise to Bronya, and she was going to keep it.

Finally, Bronya wrote. "Manya, I am settled. I am finishing my studies. I even plan to marry. Come to Paris and study. We'll help you. You must make this decision; you have been waiting too long."

As Manya read Bronya's letter, a strange feeling came over her. She was not joyful but afraid and hesitant. Paris was too far away. And what would her father, brother, and sister do without her?

Manya wrote to Bronya, "I'm sorry. I can't come to Paris yet."

She returned to Warsaw. For another year, she worked and attended a secret university, the Floating University. For the first time, she was able to work in a laboratory. She loved working with real equipment. It was exciting to use chemicals and solutions and try real experiments.

Slowly, Manya's old determination returned. Despite her fear of living in a new country, learning a new language, and getting by on little money, Manya knew she could wait no longer. She was twenty-three years old and had to take a chance.

She gathered her few belongings together. "I won't be away for long, two years, maybe three. Then I'll return and we'll be together," she promised her family.

At the train station, Manya's family hugged her tight. "Work hard. Come back soon," they called as she waved good-bye. Then she stepped into the fourth-class carriage, the only train compartment she could afford.

For three days, she sat on a hard stool as the train jerked along the tracks through Poland, Germany, and France. Her bones ached, and she huddled under her blanket at night, shivering with cold.

Many numbing hours after she'd left her family in Poland, the train pulled to a stop. Manya's heart beat fast as she stared out the window.

She was finally in Paris!

It was so beautiful and so terrifying.

But Manya had little time to think. There were so many things to get used to in Paris: speaking French, living on little money, traveling alone through a foreign city, meeting new people, and listening to lectures at the world-famous Sorbonne University in a hall full of men.

For the first time in her life, Manya was on her own. There were no Russian rules telling her what she could say or do. She finally had the freedom to study science. She could speak her mind and become a scientist, just as she'd dreamed.

Manya worked day and night at her studies at the Sorbonne. She worked hard at improving her French. She was determined to make the most of this chance. When her exams were over, Manya Sklodowska ranked first in science and second in math. She was one of only twenty-three women studying science.

When she accepted her awards at graduation, she used her new French name, Marie. But despite her new name and her success in Paris, she still held Poland close to her heart.

One day she knew she'd return and help establish a place where scientists, women as well as men, could study.

Marie, as she was now known, was so busy studying and working in Paris that she had little time to make friends. But then she was introduced to a shy scientist named Pierre Curie.

Pierre liked Marie immediately. He liked her devotion to science and her independent spirit. He never thought he'd meet a woman who shared his love of science.

For a while, they worked side by side, absorbed in their own projects. They discussed their excitement with their work, but they were both too shy to speak about their feelings for each other. One day, though, Pierre could wait no longer. "Marie," he said, "I want you to be my wife."

Marie knew she cared for Pierre, but she'd promised to return to Poland and her family. She turned him down.

But Pierre refused to give up. He loved Marie. They had to be together. He wrote Marie letters telling her how wonderful it would be if they could work together and share their lives. He even offered to move to Poland and continue his work there with her. Perhaps it was this offer that finally made Marie realize how much she loved Pierre and how much she wanted to spend her life with him.

In July 1895, in a simple country ceremony, Marie married Pierre. After a short honeymoon bicycling through the beautiful French countryside, they returned to Paris. By now, Marie knew she had made the right decision. Pierre was kind, caring, and devoted to her and to science.

In 1897, Marie gave birth to a daughter, Irène, but even that didn't keep her from her work for long. As soon as she could, she returned to her scientific experiments with Pierre.

Marie and Pierre were fascinated by the scientist Henri Becquerel's work with an element called uranium. Becquerel noticed that a mysterious energy emanated from uranium ore. The energy was so powerful that it conducted electricity and blackened photographic plates even when they were wrapped in heavy cardboard.

Marie and Pierre were convinced that there was an undiscovered new element inside uranium ore producing these effects. They called this new element radium. But radium was just a theory, an idea. They had to prove it existed. And to do that, they had to perform experiments that required careful work, painstaking analysis, and a large space. Where could they work? The only space they could find was a damp, poorly heated, dilapidated shack.

"If that's the only space," said Marie, "we'll take it!"

Hour after hour, day after day, they toiled in the shack, patiently analyzing piles and piles of pitchblende, a uranium mineral ore. In winter they shivered from the damp and cold, and in summer they sweltered from the heat, but they never stopped working. They were so absorbed in their search for answers, little else mattered.

Sometimes they had to work in the courtyard because the shack had no chimney to carry off smoke and poisonous gases. It was unpleasant and uncomfortable, yet Marie wrote that she spent the best and happiest years of her life in that shack.

Year after year, they struggled. After long hours of work, Marie and Pierre would go home to make dinner and care for their daughter. It was exciting to watch Irène learn to walk and talk.

Finally, after four back-breaking years of constant effort, Marie and Pierre discovered two new elements! They called one radium and the other polonium, after Marie's beloved Poland. Scientists around the world were astounded by their discoveries. Soon everyone was talking about the Curies and the amazing new element radium.

In 1903, Marie and Pierre Curie shared the Nobel Prize for physics with Henri Becquerel. Marie became the first woman to win the prize in any field. But she was too sick to attend the prize ceremony in Stockholm, Sweden. The horrible working conditions in the shack, lifting and hauling the heavy pitchblende, and most of all, handling radium had exhausted Marie and Pierre and damaged their health.

But still, they continued working.

In 1904, Marie gave birth to their second child, Eva. By now, she was constantly tired and Pierre suffered the aches and pains of rheumatism. They suspected that radium might be contributing to their illnesses, but they never realized how poisonous it was. Pierre was so unconcerned, in fact, that he even carried a test tube of radium in his pocket to show his friends. And still they kept working.

Then one rainy April day in 1906, Pierre was rushing home after a meeting. The traffic was heavy as he ran across the street, and he didn't see a horse-drawn carriage lurching toward him. With all the traffic and rain, the driver didn't see Pierre either. In an instant, he was struck by the wagon and killed.

Pierre's death devastated Marie. How could she face life without her husband, her friend, her partner in science? How could she cope with two small daughters? How could she continue her work?

But despite her deep sadness, Marie kept going. She was determined not to abandon the work she and Pierre cherished. And when the Sorbonne offered her a position as an assistant lecturer, she said yes. It was the first time in the university's 650-year history that a woman had been asked to teach science.

In 1911, Marie Curie was awarded a second Nobel Prize, this one in chemistry. With this second award, she became the first person ever to win two Nobel Prizes.

Then, in 1914, the First World War broke out in Europe. Thousands of soldiers were being wounded, and Marie knew there was no X-ray equipment close to the battlefields to diagnose their injuries. She'd lectured on X-rays and knew how they worked and how useful they could be. Although Marie disliked asking people for help, in this case she did so without hesitation. She asked all the wealthy people she knew to loan her vehicles that could be fitted with X-ray machines. She then arranged for drivers and technicians to bring the converted vans to the battlefields.

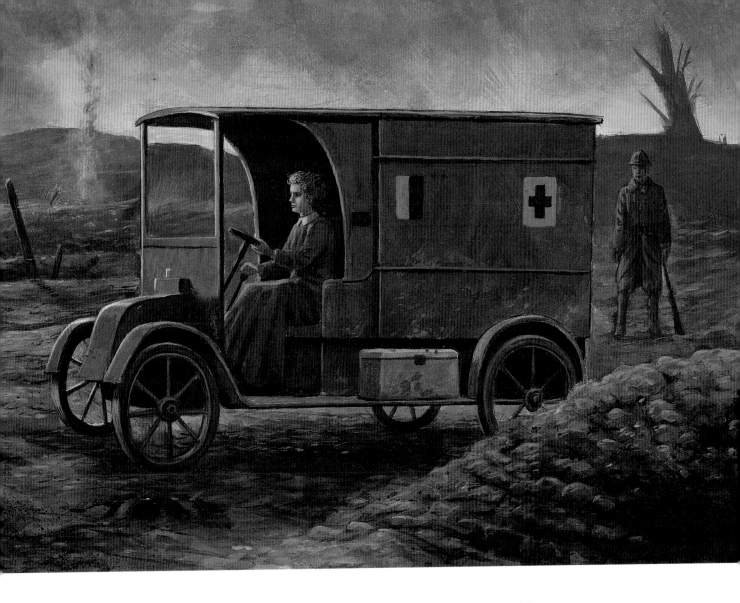

Marie even learned to drive herself. And despite being told it was too dangerous and not proper for a woman, she drove to the front lines to operate the machines and train others to do the same. By the end of the war, X-rays had speedily diagnosed the injuries of thousands of soldiers and saved countless lives.

Marie was exhausted, but she returned to her experiments in the laboratory. She also began to work for the League of Nations, an organization that tried to find peaceful solutions to conflicts between nations. And despite her busy schedule and failing health, she never forgot her promise to create a scientific institution in her beloved Poland. In 1932, she traveled home for the last time to officially open the Radium Institute in Warsaw.

When she returned to Paris, Marie was delighted to learn that her daughter Irène, who had followed in her mother's footsteps, was on the brink of exciting scientific discoveries with her husband, Frédéric Joliot. Like Marie and Pierre, Irène and Frédéric were partners in life and science. In 1935, they were also both awarded the Nobel Prize.

But Marie would not live to see her daughter win the prize. After many years of pain and weakness caused by her exposure to radium, she died on July 4, 1934. She was buried in France beside her beloved Pierre. At her graveside, her brother, Josio, and her sister, Bronya, sprinkled a handful of Polish soil over her coffin. They knew that's what their sister, Manya Sklodowska, would have wanted.

❦

For a minute after Mama finished her story about Marie Curie, we were both quiet. Then I said, "Mama, may I take your book of photographs of old Warsaw to school? I want to show my class where I come from. I want to tell everyone about Manya, a Polish girl like me who came to a new country, learned a new language, and became a great scientist."

"Everyone? Even that mean boy, Jimmy?" asked Mama, smiling.

"Especially Jimmy," I said. And then I gave Mama a hug and ran off to do my homework.

Important Dates in Marie Curie's Life

1867   Manya Sklodowska is born in Warsaw, Poland, on November 7. She's the youngest of five children.

1878   Manya's mother dies of tuberculosis.

1883   Manya graduates first in her high-school class.

1884   She spends a year in the country.

1885   Manya's sister Bronya goes to Paris to study. Manya begins work as a governess in the Polish countryside.

1891   Manya enrolls at the Sorbonne University in Paris.

1893   Now called Marie, she ranks first in her class in physics.

1894   She graduates with second honors in mathematics.

1895   Marie marries the scientist Pierre Curie in France.

1897	She gives birth to a daughter, Irène.
1898	Pierre joins Marie in her search for radium. They conduct experiments in a Paris shack they convert into a laboratory.
1902	Marie and Pierre Curie isolate radium in the laboratory.
1903	The Curies are awarded the Nobel Prize in physics.
1904	Marie gives birth to her second daughter, Eva.
1906	Pierre Curie is killed in a traffic accident.
1911	Marie receives a second Nobel Prize. This time, the award is in chemistry. She is the first person to receive two Nobel Prizes.
1914	The First World War breaks out. Marie helps bring X-ray equipment to the battlefront, saving many lives.
1932	She dedicates the Radium Institute in Warsaw.
1934	Marie Curie dies of illness caused by radium poisoning. She is buried beside her husband, Pierre, in France.

"We must believe that we are gifted for something and that this thing must be attained."
—Marie Curie